A BUG'S DAY

A Butterfly's Day

by Elizabeth Neuenfeldt
Illustrated by Claudia Marianno

BLASTOFF! MISSIONS

BLASTOFF! MISSIONS, AN IMPRINT OF BELLWETHER MEDIA BY FLUTTERBEE

Blastoff! Missions takes you on a learning adventure! Colorful illustrations and exciting narratives highlight cool facts about our world and beyond. Read the mission goals and follow the narrative to gain knowledge, build reading skills, and have fun!

Traditional Nonfiction

Narrative Nonfiction

Blastoff! Universe

MISSION GOALS

- FIND YOUR SIGHT WORDS IN THE BOOK.
- LEARN WHAT A BUTTERFLY DOES IN A DAY.
- LEARN WHERE A BUTTERFLY LAYS ITS EGGS.

This edition first published in 2027 by Bellwether Media, Inc.

Library of Congress Cataloging-in-Publication Data

Names: Neuenfeldt, Elizabeth author | Marianno, Claudia, illustrator. Title: A butterfly's day / by Elizabeth Neuenfeldt ; illustrated by Claudia Marianno.
Description: Minneapolis, Minnesota : Bellwether Media, Inc, 2027. | Series: A bug's day | Includes bibliographical references and index. | Audience: Ages 5-8 | Audience: Grades 2-3 | Summary: "Vibrant illustrations accompany information about butterflies. The narrative nonfiction text is intended for students in kindergarten through third grade."-- Provided by publisher.
Identifiers: LCCN 2026001540 (print) | LCCN 2026001541 (ebook) | ISBN 9798898800857 (library binding) | ISBN 9798898802097 (ebook)
Subjects: LCSH: Butterflies--Behavior--Juvenile literature | Butterflies--Juvenile literature
Classification: LCC QL544.2 .N48 2027 (print) | LCC QL544.2 (ebook)
LC record available at https://lccn.loc.gov/2026001540
LC ebook record available at https://lccn.loc.gov/2026001541

Editor: Betsy Rathburn Designer: Laura Sowers

Printed in the United States of America, North Mankato, MN.

This is **Blastoff Jimmy**! He is here to help you on your mission and share fun facts along the way!

Table of Contents

A New Day

JIMMY SAYS

A monarch butterfly spends up to two weeks in its chrysalis.

The sun is rising. A new day has begun!

A female butterfly hangs inside its **chrysalis**. It is time to start its day!

The butterfly breaks out of its chrysalis.

It opens its wings and lets them dry. Soon it will be ready to fly!

Taking Flight

The butterfly flies through a forest in search of flowers.

Will it find some flowers with **nectar** in them?

predator

Suddenly, a bird flies nearby. Look out!

The butterfly quickly flies in different directions. It gets away from the **predator**. Phew! That was close!

The butterfly spots
a field of flowers.

It flies to a flower. It drinks nectar from the flower with its **proboscis**. Yum!

The butterfly **flutters** from flower to flower. It carries **pollen** to different flowers.

This helps more flowers grow!

pollen

Soon, it is time to look for a **mate**.

There is a male on that milkweed plant. The female butterfly flies closer.

The female butterfly lays eggs on the milkweed plant.

Soon the eggs break open. **Caterpillars** come out. They eat a lot of milkweed leaves!

Moving On

Now the butterfly is **migrating** south.

The sun is going down. It is time to rest. The butterfly joins other monarchs in a tree. Good night!

All About Butterflies

Body Parts

Things Seen

flowers

pollen

eggs

Glossary

caterpillars–wormlike young butterflies

chrysalis–a hard shell that forms around a caterpillar while it changes into a butterfly

flutters–flies by moving its wings quickly

mate–a partner

migrating–traveling from one place to another

nectar–a sweet liquid that comes from plants

pollen–a fine dust found in plants that is carried to other plants of the same kind to make seeds

predator–an animal that hunts other animals for food

proboscis–a long, tube-shaped body part on a butterfly that is used to take in nectar

To Learn More

AT THE LIBRARY

Grack, Rachel. *Monarch Butterflies.* Minneapolis, Minn.: Bellwether Media, 2024.

Kenney, Karen Latchana. *All About Butterflies.* Minneapolis, Minn.: Jump!, 2024.

Ruby, Rex. *A Butterfly Grows.* Minneapolis, Minn.: Bearport Publishing Company, 2026.

ON THE WEB

FACTSURFER

Factsurfer.com gives you a safe, fun way to find more information.

1. Go to www.factsurfer.com.
2. Enter "a butterfly's day" into the search box and click 🔍.
3. Select your book cover to see a list of related content.

BEYOND THE MISSION

> WHAT FACT FROM THE BOOK DID YOU THINK WAS THE MOST INTERESTING?

> DRAW A BUTTERFLY. WHICH BODY PARTS DO YOU THINK ARE MOST IMPORTANT?

> WHICH PART OF A BUTTERFLY'S DAY DO YOU THINK IS MOST IMPORTANT?

Index